In Your Deep Waters

By

Joanna Lemus

Table of Contents

The truth lies with us.
Harder than losing someone is finding
ourselves again.
Here is to us, the broken ones

I. Notion of Love

In your waters, I felt a love higher than any tsunami.
I couldn't escape it, even if I tried.

& our world oceans apart once aligned
An attraction so powerful that created a high
tide in us
Until our lowest tide arrived, we then lost the
meaning of our once-aligned world

It was the kind of love that made me leave my whole world behind. Risking it all for the notion of love, the notion of us, the notion of you, and there I went 7777 miles away from home, across the pacific ocean and all for the notion of you.

She had the warmest smile
Yet the coldest heart.

Flaws are what make us fall deeper in love
with souls.

With flaws and all, I continued to adore
but I adored her just a little too much
that I forgot what it felt like falling deeper in
love with my soul

I dived into her waters
without knowing it would wholly consume
me
and the waves never brought me back to
shore.

I carry your heart everywhere with me, and
as heavy as it weighs,
I refuse to place it back down.

In all your empty spaces, I made my little loving home.

Love, at its finest of complexities,
still makes our world go round

We didn't break.

We shattered.

& all the fragments of our love dug deeper into our flesh, crushed our bones, and left only the scars to tell our story

She made you hate everything that existed about you and me.

That's how the end of us really started.

It's not that I didn't notice the disconnection.
It was that I was too afraid to see my world
without you.

She had already changed her mind
and I was done begging for her love

Always knew

But acted indifferent

To all the things you ignored

And lied to my face

When all along, it was someone else

As you formed my replacement

You always knew

I
Turned a blind eye to
Every
Single
Red
Flag

What I didn't know couldn't hurt me until it
broke me.

2 am while half asleep, I felt you awake
Even though my back was turned on you
As your hands typed away, I knew it was
Someone else's attention you craved at 2 am.

I blamed the change of pace,
When truly, the pace shed light
To the darkness within you.

The devil in her eyes
& I stayed to learn her lessons

My silent screams
Kept me awake most nights.
I could feel my blood rushing through my
veins
Thoughts of you falling for someone else
Made the world inside my heart collapse.
Until I could no longer keep my screams
silent.
They finally soared.

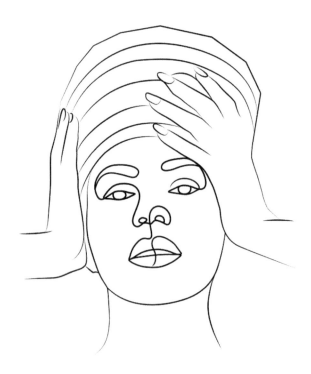

I was guarded near the end
Because all my intuitions came to be.
She told me I was manifesting something that
would never be
To my face, she lied, and I believed
And when my intuitions surfaced, she knew
she had to make me flee.

This person made you see new colors
That made you forget about the rainbow
That was already yours.

To find peace in the meaning of our
breaking.
I spent hours reading, and it all made me feel
empty.
While I opened my heart, you had already
shut yours

In her, you found similarities.
In me, you found differences.
You forced me out of your preferences.
I didn't want to force you to love me any
longer

III. Demise of You & Me

We are left to carry the burdens of the whys,
who's, and what-ifs.
But unfortunately, some endings are definite,
and the pain of never having that same love is
an enduring pain of a lifetime.

Maybe it was the forced lockdowns
In our confined place that turned our waters
dark

And yes, your darkness did end up pouring
onto me
Just like you said it would, but all my
insecurities stemmed
From the absence of your unreciprocated
love.

Treading your waters because I was too
afraid to learn how to swim without you

Even though I wasted my love on someone so undeserving of me,
I would do it all over to feel anything again.

Bitter Ending.
Far from who we were as people.
We were far too deep in our egos
And our pride got the best of you and me.

Our breaking made me feel insane.

Getting out of the crazy feeling when your world goes upside down is one of the most real life tests.

I believed hurting her back would heal the pain
But in turn, I began to believe I was to blame
And it was the guilt that almost took me.
It took an army of people to make me understand
I needed to stay to rewrite a new version of my life
Where I was never meant to be left feeling insane.

Time is the only thing we can never get back, and it's the only thing we want.

When people pass away, we say how we wish we had more time. We made the moments count, regardless of our time together cut short. I just wish we had more time.

I wanted to stay
But how could I
When I could no longer recognize the face

Some days, I feel like I'm walking through molasses.
Foggy, blurred, and all is weighing heavy on me.

I often wonder if we were never truly meant
to end.
If perhaps, we had placed our differences
aside
And broken a little less than how we left.

The panic attack at 1a.m really got the best of me.
As my arms and legs went numb, I felt uncontrollably ill inside.
I kept on thinking if I would make it out alive.
I had no choice but to leave

Regardless of how dreadful it all left us,
I wish us both nothing but peace.

We may be vulnerable and flawed
Yet we will reach the best of our individual
potentials

I waited for a love like ours
When it was no longer there, I felt dead than
alive.

Being alive is more than just being alive; it's
about staying sane in a world of deadly
people.

Some people leave our lives because they no longer need us.
These people will never find true happiness, and their cycles will leave them behind.
These people will never find true happiness.

The criticism after a breakup makes it all inside our minds feel congested.

How could anyone doubt if I ever loved her for leaving quickly? To those that were quick to remove me from their lives and to the ones that continued to cause pain with remarks, I actually thank you because it showed me that no one ever truly took the time to get to see my true heart, and I no longer felt the need to reassure the world around me if it was breaking me apart.

I felt less of a human because of these words. To succumb to these beliefs was my true failure because I'm not your words.
I am human, and I am learning.

It's crazy how our lives can go from one end of the happiness spectrum to complete depression.

What is even crazier is how we cope on our own with it all weighing heavy on us.

Take it day by day.

They will try to break you down to the core,
Just never forget in the process how to guide
yourself to stability.

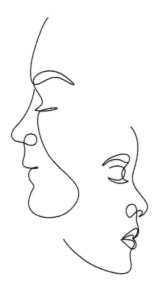

Some days feel like I'm reliving the
nightmare.
Go to bed with anxiety
Wake up with anxiety.
Until I, one day, get rid of this nightmare I
continue to replay.

Therapy teaches me to continue writing my wrongs.
To allow for the guilt and shame to not ruin what is left of me.
Apologizing to myself for the things I didn't know were right or wrong in a moment of desperation of loss and rejection.

Adding fuel to the fire,
There I was, taking back the only things I felt would make her feel the rage, from the music files to the gifts to our future plans placed away in a bin.

Therapy teaches me to continue writing my wrongs.

We all have our traumas. The need to feel safe is innate, yet we forget that our traumas don't define us as we become older.

In the process of loving you
You had already begun to unlove me.

Devil on our shoulders,
We became the ugliest version of each other

To those stuck in one-sided relationships:

I hope you can muster the energy to realize that you deserve so much better than what you stay for.

IV. Healing Waters – The Mending

Do not allow for the healing to become your identity.
Let the healing be your guide into a better version of yourself.
Allow yourself to feel, allow yourself to be soft.

I built a lighthouse to
Withstand the storm

Do not allow what hurts you to haunt you.

It's inevitable losing the people we care and love for.
Everyone in our lives serves a purpose and
And some people can only stay for a few seasons.

The nightly laments are keeping me alive.

Mending is not just healing in a soft way.
It is anger. It is bottled emotions. It is raw.
Most days, I cry at the thought of us, but
Some days, I scream into my pillow to focus
on the pain.

Rainy car rides, singing at the top of your lungs to some of Adele's music just hits different.

P.S. I still yell at the top of my lungs when our song comes on

I don't want the old me back
I don't even want a new me.

But understanding that rebirth is necessary
when healing could sometimes be triggering.
As if I am supposed to know what direction I
should head into when we are all just wanting
to be loved out of all things.

This is still the unhealed version of me.

As much pain that comes with losing you,
I think the healing hurts the most.

Between reliving the memories of us and the
words that stayed engraved in my mind.

I want to dive into healing waters to clear me
from the curse that made me love you so
fondly

Mending is truly unbalanced

Found my lowest moments with intrusive
thoughts that would drain me.
And also found my highest self among falling
in love with becoming
Something more than dwelling in the past.

We don't talk enough about the things that give us gratitude, so here is to our
pets, therapists, gym trainers, coffee, food, friends, and family, the real-time healers.

A little reminder:

YOU are your biggest fan. YOU will succeed.
YOU will love again.

I can't swim in deep waters, so when I found myself in your waters, I just kept on treading and going nowhere. I was happy being stagnant.

In your deep waters, I always felt like I was never enough
Yet, I needed your waters to help me understand the meaning of love and how to let go and begin again at my own pace.

When I emerged from this body of water, I called my tears. I began to move, and every muscle, especially my heart, just knew that it could no longer stay stagnant.

In case your mind feels negative today:

I love you; we got this. Remember that
person that once smiled so big it made
everyone around them inferior? That will be
you. Give yourself the time and space to
regain.

Broken and Sad

Wishing that we turned the pages to our next chapter into something more than the destruction we left behind.

My heart still struggles to rip you out.
But it's working on it

I am a collection of experiences bounded together.
I am not what my trauma has placed me in.
I am not what others have perceived of me.
I am waking up every day and choosing me.

Erasing the last of our photos, videos, and
messages is soul-crushing.
I went through every memory, and I began to
Smile, cry, laugh, and every emotion
continues to pour out of me.
In another lifetime, we stay to watch our
wildest dreams come true.

Turning my dreams into moments now.
I don't want to miss you anymore
And before I love another, it's safe to say that
you will
Be the only one to take all my heart could
ever do.

But maybe one day, I'll find myself not
thinking of you
Moving on towards the things that fill my
heart again.

Whenever there is an ending to a friendship
or relationship
It feels like we truly lose a part of our
identity.

Stripped away from what was once our daily
life
It's at times hard to bear in mind that at
some point, we will have
To recreate new memories, new laughs, new
worlds with other people.
A new identity, but this time, making it about
ourselves.

Everyone and everything makes me feel so lonely.
I used to be able to gravitate towards wanting to be around people
Or moving quickly. This is different. I'm learning that being alone is the best remedy.

My heart, mind, soul, and body are not ready to let you fully go. Some days, I wake up and have no will to live. Then I look at our fur child, and in many ways, I'm reminded that being alive is the most beautiful blessing, and if I can give one soul a happy life, then I will.

Our time with people is something we
can never get back, feels all like nothingness
in the end.

It felt like I wasted the best years of my love,
and here I am, reconstructing
my heart to find meaning down memory
lane.

Those little moments of progress when we
feel like we are healing.

No one talks about the fear of holding on to
the idea of what once
made you feel that a forever existed.

That first day or night, the tears don't roll
down your cheeks; these moments feel like
victories within us.

If you're reading this and going through your
life challenges, know that every little moment
is a part of this progress to your healing.

There is no rush and time limit to all the
things that are yet to happen in your life,
which will bring you pure joy.

We need to get better at cultivating healthy relationships with our minds.
The amount of time we spend fascinated by others compared to ourselves is quite ghastly.

Most of us indeed long for a partner to love since there truly is quite no better feeling than growing beside a soul that shares our equal values.

But before we devote ourselves entirely to a being, what do we know about ourselves? We hardly ever take the time to shift that focus on who we are individually, and that's where we suffer in our relationships and heartbreaks.

Every day, I learn about breaking a cycle of reshaping our mindset and understanding we cannot make other people love us, and nobody owes one another closure.
Ultimately, creating our closure, in reality, is what we should strive for.

The healing truly never ends; it's a cycle, and it takes an army inside our hearts to build up the courage again in letting down the walls to fall in love with ourselves.

It's time we cultivate a healthier relationship with our minds, and the rest will follow.

This life is ethereal.
Some days just feel heavier than others, and
that's okay.

What is most important is striving for all the
little things that
Bring us pure joy.

I know this sadness will slightly always
remain,
But I'm excited to see where we go from here.

If this is the path the universe has chosen
Then I will allow for this healing to
commence

I used to waste all my 11:11 wishes about hoping you would feel bad for the healing I was left with

But I've come to realize that I would rather manifest good over bad if it meant that we could both find peace in our ending.

To the goodbye we never had, I hope this one helps us both.
Even though our tides have turned, you were my highest form of love.

11:11 pm - Los Angeles, CA

Acknowledgement

To my parents, thank you for loving me unconditionally and taking me in when I was at the lowest point in my life with arms wide open. I Love You

To my sister, I appreciate you for always keeping that sister's intuition strong and for your continuous love and support. You are my real-life superhero.

To all my friends, each and every one of you has smothered me with love and appreciation my entire life, and I would not be me without you.

To my fur child, Leo, when I began to think I had no will to live, the thought of giving you the best life truly saved me.

To all of my readers, I can't thank you enough for taking the time to read my work. My appreciation for your existence is beyond words. If I can leave you with any message in life, it is to go and do all the little things that bring you pure joy.

"Always strive to leave people and the world better than you found them."
Sincerely,
Joanna Lemus